SINLESS

BY: FALYNN PINA

Copyright ©2022 Falynn Pina
Published by Live Limitless Media Group
Info@livelimitlessmedia.com

Falynn Pina Contact Information:
Email: falynn@falynnpina.com

Printed in the United States of America
Cover Design by: Adam I. Wade
Cover Photo by: DeMorris Marable
ISBN: 978-1-952903-26-7
Library of Congress Number: 2022915405

DEDICATION

This book is dedicated to all the women around the world who are no longer choosing silence; but instead are using their voices, telling their stories and freeing themselves from silent suffering, diminished self-worth and toxic attachments. I wrote this book for you. Know you are not alone and your voice matters.

ACKNOWLEDGEMENTS

I would like to thank my spirit guide for always protecting and guiding me. For holding my hand through all of the uncharted territories this life has bestowed upon me.

Those who continue to strive when the tough gets going, those who choose kindness over cruelty, I thank all of the women who have not only survived divorce, but had the courage to forgive themselves after choosing self-worth. My best friend, Jaylan, for always having my back even when it may be at your own detriment; you put me and the children first. Your desire for self-growth is unmatched. I'll find you in every lifetime.

I'd like to thank my children, even with all of my imperfections, for choosing me to be their mommy.

The Pina Crew who continue to show devoted love and compassion for my family.

AUTHOR NOTE

The events and experiences detailed here are all true and have been faithfully rendered as they have been remembered. In certain instances and scenes, the names and identifying details of the people and places involved have been changed for privacy's sake.

Though conversations, concepts and account of details come from my keen recollection of them, they are not written to represent word-for-word documentation; rather, I've retold them in a way that evokes the real feeling and meaning of what was said, what happened and my interpretation of events.

TABLE OF CONTENTS

EPIGRAPH

"He who is without

sin may cast the *First Stone*"

~John 8:7

PROLOGUE

I can't say that I'm the most religious person. I can't recite many bible scriptures, and I haven't always done everything right. I've had my share of poor decisions followed by hard lessons, and I have had to recover from loss, heartbreak, abuse, betrayal and disappointment. Like many other women who wake up every day and choose to exhibit courage while also carrying the burden of everything they've been through...or being brave enough to start their day with a smile, after crying all night. The women who struggle to find the emotional space to heal, cry, release and reimagine their lives when the convenient thing to do is remain the same. For the women who have been resilient enough to survive, but are now embracing the idea that they can thrive, experience joy, be loved properly and live a life of peace, alignment, luxury and fulfillment. A life that isn't driven by fear, triggers, survival, toxicity or settling…to the women who are no longer remaining silent for the sake of keeping the peace, the moms who are doing the sometimes-hard *heart work* to heal so that they can break the cycle of trauma in their families, the women who are prioritizing self-love, self-awareness, self-acceptance and self- care, because they are learning to truly value themselves. To the women who understand that true wealth is reflected in things that money can't buy, the women who understand that a life of luxury is not limited to material possessions, but it's the priceless gift of actually loving the life that you get to wake up to.

To women like me….I wrote this book for you. It's my way of standing up for us when we're judged, misunderstood and harshly criticized by those who slander our names but don't know our stories. I know what it's like to crave affection from people who are incapable of caring for your emotional needs. I know what it's like to have your childhood trauma cause you to fall victim to people and relationships that deplete you and feed off of your diminished sense of self-worth. I know what it's like to be stripped of your truth because you chose *peace* over drama and *distance* over disrespect.

Millions of people witnessed one of the most difficult transitions of my life. Divorce is hard, but having your heartbreak and humiliation on display for millions of people on national television is a different type of hurt. When your lifestyle and marriage is being cast on a major network, your pain is on public display. The problem with broadcasting your life to the world is being subject to other peoples unwarranted criticism, premature judgment, slander, lies, rumors, assumptions and false narratives. When the news of my husband getting engaged to one of my castmates hit the social media streets, I was bombarded with media clips, articles, blogs and comments about their engagement. I don't know what was more humiliating…finding out online from a blog, or not having the opportunity to hurt in private. The only way to get away from the noise was to completely log off and plug into my personal healing. There were so many new things happening in my life while other things were ending. I was getting a very public divorce, walking away from my role on The Real Housewives of Atlanta franchise, falling in love with a new version of myself, discovering healthy relationships, and healing from years of living out of alignment with my values all while pregnant. I was decluttering my life and ignoring the chatter for the sake of healing. My healing required detachment from dysfunction, so I gracefully bowed out of the battle to combat with chaos, conflict, criticism and negative conversations.

But what I've realized is that while silence keeps the peace around you, it sometimes creates a war within you. I was keeping quiet because to be completely honest, I was still processing, hurting, healing and getting clear. I was embracing healthy love while releasing toxic attachments. I was getting to know the version of myself that was willing to go against the grain of other people's opinions, give myself what I really needed and truly valued in life…not just what looked good. I was doing what felt right in my heart, what felt safe in my soul, and what I wanted to do. I was no longer allowing other people's ideas of what I should do to drive my destiny. I was reclaiming the driver's seat in my life and allowing faith to be my guide… the silence that once felt so safe, started to feel more like a sin. In my quiet place where I had time and space to reflect, my voice was unveiled and the need to unmute myself became alarming. It's not that I needed to defend myself, prove anyone wrong or meet slander with spite. You see, my desire to unleash my truth is not about confrontation. It's about giving myself the gift of transformation and hopefully inspiring other women to do the same.

When we share our stories, other women realize that they are not alone. When we open up about our experiences and talk about what we've gone through, it reveals to others that growth, change and life after love and loss *is possible*. When we share our stories, we reclaim our personal narratives and we silence the voices that try to convince us that we don't matter, we're not enough, or that we're not deserving of good things.

I'm sharing my story because holding it captive does a disservice to the women who will be empowered to walk away, start over, and dream again. I am breaking my silence, liberating myself from shame and choosing to be fearless. Owning your story gives you the power to create brand new chapters. You realize that the pen is in your hand, and you can choose to live, love and experience life differently.

Don't allow your fear of judgment to cause you to shrink to the level of other people's opinions. The truth is, none of us have lived a life void of error. We all have pages in our lives that we wish we could rewrite or even rip out. To be frank, others can have an opinion, but you don't have to give a fuck.

I've heard and read so many ridiculous things about me online that were vicious, vile, untrue and straight up made up. I've heard it all, "Falynn fumbled the bag, she's dating the help, she got caught cheating with the butler and is carrying his child, she has four children with four different men, she let someone steal her man" and the list goes on....but even in the face of backlash and false narratives, I knew the truth and I knew that I would share it when I was ready. It wouldn't be a retaliation, but more so a revelation of the real me, the healed me....the best and most authentic version of me.

So, whether others like you or not, never apologize for being who you are. I mean, who among us can cast the first stone? It's not your job to protect the reputation of those who have hurt you and you don't have to be boxed in by what other people think. Their words can't wound you when you don't need their validation to define you. Life becomes better when you are bold enough to be whoever the fuck you want to be while sharing your truth without regret. There is freedom that comes with being blameless, but the truth is... none of us are *Sinless*.

CHAPTER
ONE
THE FIRST STONE

*"In order to truly understand someone's
story, you would have to start from the
beginning"*

I was no stranger to toxicity. I mean, to be honest,
dysfunction and abuse were so familiar that my
tolerance for it became common. It was the foundation
from which I had learned to survive. It was introduced to
me early on like a small child and their favorite blanket;
except for me, it wasn't a warm and fuzzy comfort item,

it was layers of thinking I'd have to unlearn, wounds I'd have to heal from, loved ones I'd have to forgive and apologies I'd learn to live without.

I was born in 1989 in Panama City, FL. The story is told that my parents were teenagers who were forced to get married by their parents after learning of my mother's pregnancy, but who truly knows. After having my sister and I, they separated shortly after their forced marriage. When I was around 9 months old, my mother packed up and moved to Atlanta Georgia where she raised my siblings and I.

By the time I was three, my mother started dating again and ended up finding love. Her new companion was the very first father figure that I had. He cherished the ground my sister and I walked on. It is said that a girl's first love is her father, but what happens when the first man you ever loved abuses your mother?

Witnessing my mother's ongoing physical and verbal abuse would be just the beginning of my trauma.

By the time I was eight, my mother eventually left him and we moved into my uncle's basement. By this time, our party of three had grown to four. My mother and new step-father had a son and my sister and I now had another younger brother.

Everything started off good. He was like the perfect dad. He seemed amazing for my mom. He was a musician and producer who lived a life parallel to that of a starving artist. I admired his craft, at that time in my life I dreamed of becoming a singer. My mother's relationship with him escalated quickly. He moved out of his mother's house and joined us in my uncle's basement. Even as a young girl, it was clear that my aunt and uncle weren't too fond of my mother's new husband. I didn't understand why they didn't like him but it was clear that they didn't. Their intolerance for him grew and they eventually gave my mother an ultimatum. He was no longer welcome in their home and they wanted him to move out. My mother was faced with a choice, to stay or leave with him. She chose him so we moved out and moved into a two-bedroom apartment.

By the time I was ten, he had started to spank my siblings and I. His abuse was gradual, first spankings with chopsticks and then it went from chop sticks to a miniature hand-held baseball bat. He would hit us in the center of our foreheads. If his pillows weren't adjusted properly or if we forgot to sweep, we would be hit. The wood from the bat eventually shattered from the constant hits that he would dish out. After the bat shattered, he went to Lowes and had a paddle custom made out of two-by-fours to hit us with. He would even brag about having a rubber grip designed into the handle and how the rubber grip was going to help him hit us better.

He cooked dinner every night but he rationed out our food and snacks. My mother was always at work being the breadwinner to support our family so we were always home with him. I remember the many times when my sister and I would save portions of our McDonald's

Happy Meals so that we would have food to eat later. There was this one time when my sister and I placed a portion of our Happy Meal into the refrigerator to eat later. My little brother who had gotten hungry helped himself to the rest of my burger. I was mad at him and I asked him why he had taken my burger. He replied and said it was because he was hungry. My stepfather overheard us and he came into the kitchen, lifted my little brother up by his arm and proceeded to hold him in the air and beat him with his new custom-made two-by-four paddle. That was when things went from bad to worse. That day is embedded in my memory, it was so hard to stand by and witness my five-year-old brother being beaten for being hungry. I don't think my brother has ever recovered from his abuse; he struggles to this day.

We would go to school every day hiding our abuse and our scars. I remember wondering if anyone was ever going to pay attention to us long enough to discover what we were going through, was anyone ever going to help us? Could we run away? How would we? He told us that if we ever told a soul, that we would be taken away from our mother and raped. We were afraid to speak up but we wondered and even hoped that someone would notice, speak up and save us. My sister and I had discussed running away and simply not coming home from school, but we could never leave our little brother behind. He was still so young and vulnerable. We couldn't bear the thought of leaving him alone.

No 'one spoke up and as time went on, we endured the pain and eventually we got quieter and quieter when we were among other family members. Whenever we would attend family functions, we would hope that that day would be the day that someone questioned our silence, unveiled our abuse and rescued us from the pain of it all. They must have assumed that we were just navigating the common path of puberty, and perhaps we were just in our awkward adolescents. No one seemed to know and no one said anything.

Eventually, the physical abuse would turn sexual. I was thirteen years old when he molested me. I was always a daddy's girl. I loved the idea of being loved by my father. Especially since my first dad was no longer in my life. I missed being his princess and I looked for that same feeling of comfort and protection in all of my mother's husbands. Needless to say, I was disappointed, my trust was violated and I learned the hard way that all men are not created equally.

I remember my sister coming up to me and in a faint voice saying, "Falynn, Greg, wants you." So I went downstairs and Greg asked me to come massage his leg. I agreed and I excitedly started to massage his leg. The little girl in me who craved the love and acceptance of a father figure was eager to please. He told me that he had hurt his leg and wanted me to massage the pain away. As I was massaging his legs he said, "didn't you say you were having back pain from your backpack being so heavy?" I replied, "yeah, it's been hurting." He then told me to lay down on my stomach. He started massaging my back and eventually made his way down to my backside. He began to remove my pants. I was in such shock that I couldn't get any words out. I laid there in silent shock as he began inserting his fingers into me. I grew intensely uncomfortable and I was able to muster up the words, Greg, I feel uncomfortable. He said, "Ok" and he put my pants back on. He told me that I didn't need to tell anyone what happened because once I told him that I was uncomfortable, he had stopped.

So, the next day came, it must've been a weekend because my mother was home from work. I was scared shitless but I knew I needed to tell my mom. After I told her what happened with Greg and how he had violated my young body, she took me into the restroom and told me to pull my pants down to show her exactly where he had touched me and what he had done. After showing her, she told me to go upstairs.

I remember my mother being in shock. I could tell that she was very upset but she didn't say much. She just told me to go upstairs and to not come back downstairs. I went upstairs and went straight to my room. I walked past my sister, and I didn't even tell her. I didn't have the heart to tell her because I knew it would break her heart. She always felt like it was her job to protect me and I didn't want to have to relive the pain of having to go into detail again about what happened. As I made my way into my room, I remember hearing my mother and step father yelling downstairs. They were screaming and yelling, and then it got quiet. At some point in time, they called me downstairs. I came downstairs into the living room where they were both sitting. My step father was sitting in his chair and my mother was sitting on the other couch. They were both looking at me when my mom eventually breaks the stiff silence and says, "Falynn, tell me exactly what happened." So, again I tell her everything. My step father chimed in and started switching up the story trying to convince me that I was crazy, and that it never happened. He must have been very convincing because my mother started to buy into his version of events. He even convinced her that she was there during the time of the alleged abuse and that I was laying on the floor and she was next to him at the time. My story had become some figment of my imagination and I was made to feel as though I was crazy, but deep down we all knew the truth. My mother chose to stay with him because she was threatened to have her children taken away from her. Once all of my siblings reached the age of maturity, my mother left Greg and started her life over.

Although the adult consensus on the issue was that nothing happened, my mother still implemented a new set of house rules that I would have to follow. I was no longer allowed to be in the same room with my step father alone, and I was no longer allowed to wear any shorts or clothing that revealed my body. I had to wear sweatpants and big T-shirts. In high school, he convinced my mother that my sister and I were too fast and as a result we didn't need to have any friends, so we weren't allowed to have any friends. We were not allowed to go outside and we had to keep all the windows in the home closed.

Some of the kids at school started noticing that we never talked to or engaged with the other students. They noticed how much we would hide by wearing long sleeves and hoodies even in the summer heat. I don't know how, but one of my classmates retrieved my phone number. We weren't allowed to give out our phone number ever so I was petrified when they called the house and threatened to tell the authorities about the abuse they believed was happening. When they called our home, Greg answered because he was the only one who was allowed to answer the phone. Nobody was allowed to talk on the phone except for him. I knew something was wrong when I heard him yelling on the phone, saying "you little punk niggas… ya'll are kids. I'll shoot you dead nigga!" I immediately knew it was the kids who told me they found my phone number. I begged them not to call my house, at that moment I realized that they had not obliged to my heartfelt request. I remember holding my baby sister who was an infant. As I'm holding her, he rushes out of his room and storms towards me from across the hall and slapped me across my face. As I'm recovering from the hit, my mom comes up to me and she says, "give me my baby." She takes my little sister away from me, and my step father proceeds to take out his two-by-four. He beat me so bad that my head swelled and I fainted. He had beat me all over my body and my head. My head had swelled so much that I couldn't go to school for three weeks. All the kids, of course, thought I was dead. My sister was forced to stay home for a few days after the beating but she was eventually allowed to go back to school. One day when she came home after school, she approached me and whispered to me that she was going to speak up and tell someone what happened. She told me that she was going to the police, my step father was eavesdropping and when he heard her say that she was going to tell, he grabbed a dustpan stick that was nearby and beat her with it until her skull cracked. My sister's young body went into shock from the blunt force trauma to her head. I remember my mom sitting in a cold shower with my sister until she regained consciousness, and the color in her face returned. When my sister turned 17, she eventually ran away from home. I don't think she's ever forgiven herself for leaving me behind. After she left, we moved out of the two-bedroom apartment and our family continued to grow. I now had a new baby sister and two baby brothers. We all moved out of the two-bedroom apartment and into a house that my mother purchased. For some reason, after we moved into the house, things got better. My step father never hit me again. My mom was finally easing up and allowing me to have a life and friends. They felt like I was really depressed after my sister ran away, and the truth is that I was. So I guess in some weird attempt to pacify the pain of my absent sister, he allowed me to make friends. But I was so traumatized that it was very hard for me to engage with my peers. So, even though I was now allowed to meet new people, I honestly didn't even know how to so I still didn't have any friends. For the longest time they made us wear school uniforms to public school and this was a new rule they decided to lift. I was now able to start wearing regular clothes to school.

By the time I was 15 years old, I was allowed to start dating. This only meant that I was allowed to talk to a boy on the phone and at times he was allowed to come over. It was weird because I called him one day and his aunt recognized my mother's name from the caller ID. My mother had kept my father's last name. She never changed it for the sake of my sister and I. It just so happens that my boyfriend's aunt was very best friends with my biological father, who had been absent from my life since before I can remember, and she was from Panama City, Florida. Panama City is a very small and tight knit community. His aunt asked my boyfriend about me and asked to see a picture of my mother. My boyfriend didn't have a picture so he described my mother the best he could. He must've provided a very thorough description, because when his aunt returned to Florida, she met with my father and told him that she believed her nephew was dating me. I remember getting a call about a week later. I was in art class and the front office called me on the intercom into the principal's office. When I reached the office, I was told that my Aunt Linda was on the phone. Linda is my mom's sister so I immediately began to think that something terrible had happened to my mother since my mom and my aunt Linda didn't speak at all. When I made it to the office, I was told to return my aunt's call using the number that she provided. When the woman answered the phone, it wasn't my mom's sister Linda, but an unfamiliar voice who began to ask me what my middle name was. My middle name is not legal. Only my mom, dad and sister know my middle name because my mom never put it on my birth certificate. So, I said, my middle name is Jade. The woman on the phone then yelled in excitement. "It's her, It's her!" And then a man with a very deep voice got on the phone. His very first words were, "Do you know who this is?" and I immediately started crying. I said, "Yes, I know who this is' ' then in an instance the clerk from the school's front office yells at me to hang up the phone. She must've realized that my "Aunt Linda" was actually a stranger who had called the school in an attempt to locate me. My father heard the background commotion and urged me to quickly take his number down. I wrote the number down that he gave me and then the school clerk took the number from me and called my mom.

My mom told her to give me the phone number back and that it was okay. I was scared shitless because I feared that I was going to get in trouble when I got home.

Instead, when I got home, my mother asked me if I wanted to meet my father. I told her that I did want to see him and she called him to set it all up. I was so excited and he drove down to visit me two weekends in a row from Panama City to Atlanta. When I met him, I immediately noticed just how much I acted like him. Reconnecting with my father was like finally finding the missing puzzle piece of my life.

My mother noticed a major difference in me after I met my father and she asked me if I wanted to go live with him. She said I seemed down and I was no longer singing around the house. I told her no because I was afraid that if I said yes, I would get the shit beat out of me. She asked me again and this time told me to tell her the truth. So, I said, "Yes, I do. I want to go live with him." She said, "Okay, I'm going to tell you this. I'm going to call him and I'm going to tell him to come get you. When you leave tomorrow for school, you take nothing but the clothes on your back and don't ever come back to my house." My step father tried to convince me to stay by telling me that I didn't know anything about my biological father and that it would be inappropriate if I ever sat on his lap. He went on making demands saying that I could never kiss my biological father because I was too old for kisses and he didn't really know me. It was all just so much to process at 15 years old, but I was happy to leave.

My dad wasn't able to leave work to come get me for two days. So, I went and hid in one of my friend's rooms and her mom found out of course. My friend's mother was afraid of getting in trouble for harboring a runaway so she then gave me a ride to my boyfriend's house and he ended up hiding me in the basement until his dad found out. But because they were friends with my dad, he let me stay until my dad arrived. My dad ended up coming to get me and I only stayed with him for three months because it turned out that my issues with abandonment, coupled with the trauma of abuse didn't allow me to easily transition into the role of a princess that my father imagined. Our reunion was great, but my father taking full responsibility of me overnight proved to be more of a challenge than either of us imagined and our reunion bliss was cut short.

While in Panama City, I lost my virginity, fell in love with a boy who my dad thought was bad news and he put me on the first Greyhound bus back to Atlanta. By this time, my older sister who had run away had her own apartment and she allowed me to come live with her. I didn't stay with her long, she ended up kicking me out and I went to live with my best friend and her boyfriend. I was sixteen, alone and feeling unloved. I was struggling to find a place in the world where I could fit, be loved, accepted and happy.

We were all just a bunch of runaways in my best friend's apartment. One day, this boy comes rushing through the front door with his basket of laundry and basketball in hand. He was already eighteen when he moved in with us. He would become my oldest son's father.

I was sixteen and I wanted to re-enroll into school. When I went to my mother for help, she reminded me that when I left her house to move in with my father, she told me that I could never come back to her. Since I was still a minor, I couldn't enroll myself into school so I became a dropout on top of being a teen mom. I hated my mom for not supporting me, or protecting me all those years. I told her she was dead to me and I didn't talk to her for years.

I had a rocky start in life, I never received the love, care and nurturing that every child deserves. Now that I was embarking on the journey of motherhood, I felt hopeless and I feared that I didn't have the tools to nurture my baby boy but I was determined to survive. It's what I had always done, it's what I knew how to do best.

CHAPTER
TWO

OPERATING
IN SURVIVAL MODE

"The habits you created to survive will no longer serve you when it's time to thrive. Be brave enough to establish new habits, and new beliefs so that you can experience a brand-new life"

~Anonymous

I was a mom at 16 years old. My two oldest sons, Troy and Dylan, are only 14 months apart. They were conceived during a time in my life when I struggled the most. I met Troy's father while living in an apartment with a few other displaced teens. He was the cousin of the guy who owned the apartment we were all staying in. He was 18 years old and I was 16 at the time. When he moved into the apartment with us, we took a liking to one another and started dating. We were two young souls trying to survive without guidance. I ended up getting pregnant and boy did shit get real. I lost count of the times we were evicted. Being displaced while pregnant was a new level of struggle for me. My step father would ration out our meals but we would eat, no matter how little the portion, I knew that at some point in the day I would be offered food. But 16 and 100 percent responsible for myself and the life growing inside of me brought major hardship and I felt like I didn't have anyone to turn to for help. Troy's father started using drugs and alcohol to deal with the stress of it all. I remember going door to door begging my neighbors for food. Once, I even checked myself into the hospital just to get a hot meal. There were many times when we were starving and when I begged my father for money, he started sending me $50 Every three weeks. After struggling to survive with my oldest child's father, I eventually moved in with my uncle. While living with my uncle, I gave birth to my oldest son Troy. After having Troy, I moved back in with my older sister in her new apartment. This is where I met her next-door neighbor. He was a 21-year-old college student and bartender. He seemed like such a cool guy. He was passionate about his career and dedicated to his dreams of becoming a mixologist. He was such a fun person to be around. The first time we had sex the condom fell off, and I got pregnant. We didn't know one another very much when I got pregnant so he encouraged me to get an abortion. I was on the way to the clinic to get an abortion, but I lost the nerve at the last minute. When I chose to keep Dylan, his father and I tried the whole relationship thing. It felt like we were forcing the relationship for the sake of our son. It turned out that he was highly insecure. He would accuse me of cheating for singing a song on the radio that was about cheating. He would even come to my job, watch me work and accuse me of sleeping with my boss while I was pregnant. The relationship was toxic to say the very least. We were living with his parents during my pregnancy with Dylan. During arguments he would always threaten to take my baby once he was born. After I gave birth to our son, with the support of his parents, he took me to court where he fought for custody. I was 19 with two young boys and battling what was later determined to be postpartum depression. I didn't know what postpartum depression was, I just knew that my mind, body and soul all felt so very tired and drained. Waking up felt heavy and getting out of bed on many days was hard. Dylan's father and grandparents used my depression against me in court, claiming that I was an unfit parent, and the judge ruled in their favor. The same judge, however, later ordered that my son be returned to my custody 11 years later only one month after I petitioned the court. Dylan had been living with his paternal grandparents, and while I know they loved him and most likely provided a more stable environment for him at the time, they had failed to properly nurture his early childhood learning and development. After the courts reviewed his school records and discovered that he had missed 82 days of school and was learning on a second-grade level at the age of 11, they quickly allowed me to regain custody of him. After two years of homeschooling and hired tutors and various specialists, he eventually caught up and got back on track.

I met my third son, Liam's father when I was filming on set in Atlanta. He was the contracted videographer for the shoot and he was a talented creative. He seemed to be very popular on set and at the end of the shoot most of the talent on set exchanged numbers. Once he received my number, he spent a year trying to get my attention through a series of romantic gestures. We eventually started to date and the relationship turned abusive very quickly. He was both emotionally and physically abusive. He would throw knives at me, kick me, punch me and even urinated on me. Crazy as it sounds, although he was abusive, he was my first true love. Or so I thought. So, when he moved to LA to pursue his creative endeavors, I joined him to pursue my own dream at the time of becoming an actress. I was excited to see California. It felt like a dream but it turned out to be a nightmare. I didn't find out that I was pregnant with Liam until I was about four months pregnant. During a photo shoot, I met a model who seemed cool and we became close quickly. Liam's father and I began to hang out with the model. We were all creatives in LA with dreams of making it big; but then things got weird when he stopped coming home at night. I knew that he was cheating, but I stayed with him because I was pregnant and so far away from home. To be honest, I was also very naive. During that time of my life, I didn't really have much of a voice. I had grown up in a home where my voice was silenced. I didn't have a lot of freedom or agency over myself, my thoughts, my beliefs, or even the way that I dressed. I carried this timid and powerless attitude into most of my adult relationships. It proved to be a trait that allowed me to become susceptible to abuse. It caused me to be very tolerant of toxicity and made me very easy to be taken advantage of. I knew something was going on with Liam's dad and my friend. Since we were all friends, we would all hang out, but things started to feel oddly intimate between them; I would catch them coming out of the garage together, but what really took the cake was when he bought her car. I mean, I was his pregnant girlfriend and I didn't even have a car. So, when he bought her a car, it was clear that there was more to their relationship. Call me crazy, but I stayed. His excuse was that he happened to have money on him at the time and our mutual friend's father was going to pay him back. I knew things weren't adding up, but again I was young, in love and really naive. My naivety turned to rage and I had enough. I had come home and caught my friend upstairs in my bathroom. When I walked in, she was cleaning my mirror and I snapped. She had gotten way too comfortable in my intimate space. I ran downstairs to the kitchen, grabbed a knife and I threatened to kill them both. I was at my breaking point. So tired of people taking advantage of me. So tired of people lying to me and getting away with it. So tired of people hurting me, and then feeling like I didn't have a choice but to tolerate it. I was tired of people violating me. The timid girl who had allowed so much bullshit was done. I confronted them about sleeping together, and they initially denied it. He eventually told her to leave and to never come back. They would continue to date behind my back, and he would eventually leave me to be with her. I was over my California dream and so ready to get away. I gave birth to Dylan and asked my sister for money to help me leave California. Once I received the money, I hid it. My son's father comes in, searches the room, finds my stash of cash and tries to steal it away from me. We got into a huge tussle and the police were called. I was arrested and was served with a restraining order from him while in jail prohibiting me from making contact with our son. Once I was eligible for release, he posted my bail with the money that he stole from me. Once I was released, I remember walking home 12 miles in the desert dressed in the clothes that I went to jail in, which was a T-shirt. I was arrested without shoes so the release staff at the county jail gave me a pair of size 11 jail shoes to go home in. Once the judge reviewed the case, it was thrown out and charges were dropped.

Not knowing myself or my self-worth caused me to accept abuse and narcissism in many forms; and although my partners were all abusive, there was something that was comforting about the pain. Trauma was a part of my comfort zone, I never had to question what it would feel like because I knew what to expect. I mean, you cannot miss what you've never had. I never had an example of functional love. I thought narcissistic abuse was love. I had children early without ever considering that as a woman, I should have a right to choose when I'm ready to bring life into this world when I'm ready to be a mother. I had never gained personal agency in so many aspects of my life. I felt as if I didn't have a choice in many cases. I simply had to take life as it was handed to me and roll with the punches. I didn't stand in my power as a kid because I was never allowed to, I gave up my power as a young woman because I didn't know the value of it.

Living in constant survival is like living through the motions of an unbroken cycle. When I reflect on the most challenging moments of my life, I realize that the events, situations and people involved may have changed, but the root causes of my issues were the same. We often don't realize the damage of our wounds until they start to show up in other areas of our lives. As a young girl who was abandoned by her father and then abused by the men in her life who were supposed to love and protect her, I subconsciously set a very low standard for how men should treat me. My idea of love was warped. I saw love through the dysfunctional lens of the examples set before me. Love was abusive, manipulative, toxic, and often painful. I learned early on that it was normal and even acceptable to remain loyal to dysfunction and detriment. I became a homeless, high school dropout and teen mom at the age of 16. I went from surviving the most toxic form of mental, emotional, physical and sexual abuse in my home as a young girl, to living on my own and navigating life as a young mother. Survival became my default setting. It was embedded so deeply in my core that I didn't even realize I was surviving, to me I was simply living and trying desperately to make it. Back then, I didn't have the luxury of healing. I'm sure during that time I didn't truly realize that there were things I needed to heal from. I thought that no longer being under the same roof as my abuser would be the end of the pain, but trauma lingers and it hides in the crevices of our hearts and minds. So often women carry the heaviness of their inner wounds and operate under the false belief that just because the wounds are not visible to the naked eye, that they don't exist. But they do exist, and the catalyst of unhealed trauma finds a way to appear at the most inopportune times. Looking back, I can now appreciate that becoming aware of my brokenness allowed me to discover the areas in my life that required tenderness, love, care and grace fueled healing. The points of pain in my life unveiled the root cause of decisions, partners and situations that reflected the version of me that was willing to tolerate less than what I deserved. When you operate in survival you often take what you can get. Healing required me to reimagine what

I was worth through the lens of self-love, self-discovery, and personal awareness.

Simon wasn't the first man to break my heart, abandon me, lie to me, or take advantage of my vulnerability; he was simply the straw that broke the camel's back. Our widely televised and talked about relationship garnered much public attention. Public interest came with public criticism and harsh judgements. So when we were having issues in our marriage, our private affairs were for public consumption and scrutiny. Being in the public eye for any reason can come with its own level of frustration, but when your heartbreak and humiliation is on display it can negatively impact the strongest among us.

I lost count of the many DM's, instant messages, comments, blog posts and personal think pieces from strangers and others who did not know what was happening in my life behind the scenes, or the heart ache I was experiencing unbeknownst to them. My public divorce compelled me to focus on private healing. Simon's betrayal brought to the forefront all of my painful experiences with men that I thought I had pushed past. If I'm being honest, I hadn't pushed past much of it at all. My perception of love along with the toxic attachments I was attracting and tolerating caused me to relive the same dysfunction with different men. The difference between my childhood trauma, and the trauma of public humiliation during my divorce was the fact that I couldn't hide. I was finally forced to deal with parts of myself that I had neglected and, in some cases, refused to face. Choosing to gracefully bow out of defending my name and reputation online in order to focus on the greater issue at hand allowed me to create a very sacred space to come to terms with my own truth. I was a wounded woman carrying years of unchecked childhood trauma into my relationships. I was a mother struggling to create a version of parenting that I had not been blessed to experience. I was a daughter dealing with betrayal and abandonment, and I was a wife seeking unconditional love in the absence of true self love. I was the perfect catch for a narcissist's supply and I was drained from operating, nonstop, in survival mode. I looked in the mirror and realized that although my exterior represented a woman who was beautiful, inside I was living with fragments of brokenness. Money couldn't fill the voids of my abandonment, there was no amount of excursions on private jets and yachts that would mend years of mental anguish. Shopping sprees were at my leisure but there wasn't a designer bag on the market that could carry the load of the heaviness I had experienced and the residue of it all that was still lingering in my life.

Although the drama that unfolded on the TV screen was hard to live through, I survived it and it forced me to realize just how necessary it was to transition from surviving to thriving. I never truly gave myself the opportunity to be who I wanted or desired to be. I was too busy being who I needed to be in order to survive. I decided that simply surviving pain would no longer be my standard. A true win in my life would be thriving despite it all and allowing purpose to outshine all of my pain.

If you have survived hard things, I salute your resilience and your will to win in spite of all of the things designed to destroy you. I know how hard it can be to feel like your life is falling apart, but you don't have to live life in shambles. You can decide to let go of what has broken you and rebuild with what you have left. Survival may be your default setting but you don't have to stay stuck. At any point in your life you can decide that you want better. I hope that when you are at your lowest point, you decide that you deserve better. I hope that when you feel as though the weight of the world is on your shoulders, you realize that you were never meant to carry the load alone. I hope that life brings you to a place of peace with people who have your best interest at heart. I hope that you celebrate the version of you that has had to survive while you embrace the version of you who can thrive instead.

CHAPTER
THREE
THE COST OF HEALING

"Healing is a priceless art. It takes time, it takes practice and it takes love"

~Maza Dohta

W hen you decide that you want to become a better version of yourself, you will first grieve the version that you must let go. My healing process was transformative but I'd be lying if I said it was a process void of frustration, tears, anger, denial and even sadness. Before we experience the beauty of properly processed pain, we must first endure the reality of our own brokenness. Healing forces you to finally face your whole self by examining your broken pieces. I had to sit and take time to understand how abuse had framed my perception and how growing up with pain playing a leading role in my adolescence was the root cause of toxic attachments in adulthood. Without self-awareness, your trauma will define you. It will become a crutch enabling you to exist with unhealed wounds and if you're not careful, you will bleed on those who didn't cut you. It was this realization that compelled me to seek therapy. I was raising children who deserved a childhood that they wouldn't need to recover from. I wanted to be a safe place for them, I desired to be the type of mother that they would be proud of, one they could learn from, respect and be inspired by. Outside of being an improved version of myself for my children, I wanted to be better for myself. I was tired of feeling like an actress in my own life, I was no longer interested in living a life that looked good. I wanted it to feel good too.

Healing is so complex. There is nothing simple about peeling back the layers of yourself, nurturing inner wounds and choosing to change. Change takes practice, intention and deliberation. Change is an unrelenting choice to do things differently. I wanted to give my children a different childhood experience, one that was more pleasant and nurturing than what I had endured. I learned that blame was powerless in the realm of personal growth. The truth is that some of the pain you endured may not have been your fault, but ultimately healing is your own responsibility. Healing is an intimate process, it doesn't require you to receive any apologies from those who hurt you, the only requisite is that you forgive yourself and are willing to move forward. Moving forward requires that you release the need to point blame, you accept what happened and you decide to no longer allow it to *define you.*

One of the major components of my personal healing journey was learning how to effectively reestablish bonds. I had developed resentment towards my mother. I was angry that she chose my abuser over me, I was angry that she decided to stay with him after I confessed my abuse. Even with the resentment that was brewing beneath the surface, I still loved my mother. I understood her in ways that many couldn't. I believed she suffered from bi-polar depression and although at times I felt that she could have done better, healing allowed me to see that maybe she was doing her best. Healing gave me the capacity to hold compassion for those who had hurt me. I was no longer angry; I was empathetic and parts of me sympathized for her. She was a teen mom like me who was trying desperately to create a family for herself. Like me, she didn't properly assess her worth and she settled for men who were not good for her. I started to see her as a whole person navigating a very hard human experience, she wasn't just my mom, she was also a woman who was wounded and trying to raise children with unhealed inner injuries. As an adult I was able to understand some of the choices my mother made and I no longer needed her to carry the blame for my brokenness, I forgave her without needing an apology. As we worked to rebuild our relationship, it was clear that our mother-daughter bond had been severely damaged. Her version of events were very different from my perspective of my childhood. It's funny how we can have a collective experience but still have separate views of the situations we shared. Creating a healthy dynamic would require me to establish boundaries to protect my peace. Since healing is a personal choice, it can be hard to reconnect with those who have not committed to doing their own inner work. This is why being able to assert necessary boundaries is so critical to reestablishing bonds. You get to decide who you want to allow into your life. Forgiveness, nor healing require you to rebuild relationships, that part is one hundred percent your choice. My mother was worth the patience and effort required to heal our relationship, but it was important that she understood that our relationship would involve a different me with new ways of engaging. I learned how to manage my triggers and even how to avoid situations, conversations and people who triggered wounds that I was working to heal. I became selective with my time and energy by being intentional about how my mother and I would spend time. I knew that extended periods of time together was bound to lead to some sort of argument, so I would make sure that we spent limited but meaningful time together. I knew that certain conversations would become a catalyst for chaos, my mother wasn't ready to take ownership of her role in my trauma and her lack of accountability would bring me back to a place of intense anger, so I was intentional about keeping our conversations focused on my children and other things that wouldn't ignite the blaze I was working on putting out. I saved all of the hard conversations for my therapist and she helped me process things that my mother was unwilling or perhaps unable to hold space for me to express without it resulting in a fight. Healing is a series of decisions; you get to decide how you want to show up in your own life and you get to decide who gets to be a part of it.

Meditation became a daily practice. It really helped me to get in tune with my own thoughts, and it helped me to reconnect with myself. I began to see myself in a brand-new light. I took time to consider who I could be and how big I could dream in spite of what I had been through. I learned the value of my own opinion and I started making choices that were best for me without the need for validation. I started validating myself, because I was enough. I removed myself from any relationship that was not reciprocal, or those that had been established based on trauma bonds. In order to truly heal, you must release the things that hurt you. I started to prioritize my own needs and self-care became more important and intimate. My self-care extended beyond the walls of the spa. It was much more intricate than a mani, pedi or facial. Self-care included time alone with my thoughts, setting boundaries with those who I loved but needed to establish a healthy way to engage with, I had to own my own imperfections, embrace my flaws and do my shadow work. Self-care became a practice of consistently choosing my best interest unapologetically even when it wasn't easy to do. I had to learn how to love myself in a way that wouldn't allow me to accept anything less than the standard I had set for myself.

Setting a standard for how I wanted to be treated, how I wanted to be loved, the qualities I desired in a partner, traits that I was unwilling to tolerate, and even holding myself to that same standard. I changed the way I saw myself and I implemented kindness into my self-talk, I no longer judge myself harshly and I forgave myself for the decisions I made when I didn't realize my worth.

CHAPTER FOUR

SWEET SURRENDER

"Let go of your attachment to what you think should have happened. Surrender to what is and trust that you're being guided towards something more profound"

~Ash Alves

I have had my share of men who are all wrong. I wanted love but I had no idea what it was. I was looking for it in all the wrong places, and every wrong turn that I made in search of love I crashed and burned at a dead end. But when I met Simon, everything seemed to change. Simon was like my knight in shining armor. He was my saving grace. I considered him my blessing. I thought that God had finally answered my prayers by giving me the love and the life that I had been searching for my whole life. I was madly in love, I felt like I would never have to suffer or worry anymore about anything. He made me feel safe and protected. He took care of me in ways that no one ever had in my life. He was much older than me, so when we would talk about our future together, I would promise him that I would take care of him. He made me feel like the queen of his world. He would tell me that he loved me most out of all the women he had ever been with and I believed him. Simon swept me off of my feet. I was perfect for him. I was young, I was beautiful and I was vulnerable because I needed someone to save me. The safety, security, and stability that Simon provided allowed me to evolve into a mature, sophisticated, business focused woman. He was a great influence on me, and I admired his work ethic. It was because of Simon that I was able to get all of my children back. He paid for the best attorneys and supported me relentlessly during every court proceeding. I was no longer a girl in survival mode. I finally found a man who I could rest in. He contributed to much of my growth as a woman, but as I grew our relationship changed. I soon realized that he didn't have the capacity to love the evolving version of me. He needed me to be vulnerable. The more vulnerable I was, the more nurturing and available I could be for him. Simon needed me to need him, and in many ways I did. But as I started to heal and discover my worth, I began to change. I started becoming stronger and wiser and it changed the dynamic of our relationship. I could understand Simon's need to have a woman nurture him. I always thought the estranged relationship with his mother was to blame. When he was 11 years old, he was sent off to boarding school. At the age of 16 When he returned home from boarding school, his father dropped him off in the United States with only $5 in his pocket. He started working at odd end jobs to survive. We bonded over our childhood trauma and our abandonment issues. He was ambitious and determined to survive. His grit and grind paid off and he was able to amass success and wealth for himself. Loving Simon felt like having everything a girl could ever want. He was a man who had enough resources to cover every need and a man who treated me like a princess and gave me the best of the best. Losing him felt like losing my sense of safety. Being with him was the first time that I had ever had the opportunity to experience what it felt like to be safe. We were supposed to last forever but forever and the princess treatment would prove to be short lived. I was in love with the man who provided me with such a great life, I was in my soft girl era and Simon was on the search for his next Cinderella story. His infidelity was in the open. It was uncommon for me to spot a young beauty taking pictures and posting them on social media inside of one of his luxury vehicles. He went from dibbling and dabbling outside of our marriage, to straight up disappearing for weeks and months at a time.

Letting go of things that I believed and hoped would last forever was one of the hardest things I've had to do. Sometimes the things and the people we want the most are not always what we need. The idea of needing someone in itself is an indication that you are not secure within yourself. Healthy attachments should add to who you are and who you are becoming. Your relationships aren't supposed to fill your voids, instead they should complement and amplify you in areas where you are already whole. The problem with securing healthy attachments, is that too many of us are too broken to believe that they exist. Our society has normalized toxicity, ignored red flags and taught us to embrace being chosen even if it means that we lose a piece of ourselves in the process. We are taught to prioritize luxury over true love. We are programmed to believe that material comfort can take the place of sincere sanctuary within oneself, where your soul is fed, your needs are met and your personal integrity is intact.

Although the art of surrendering can be a struggle, if you focus on making room for things that fuel your dreams and goals you will eventually find your sweet spot. It took some time for me to discover the good in goodbye. When I became consciously aware that my marriage had come to an end, my immediate emotion was fear. I remember sitting on my therapist's couch when I finally stopped fighting for someone who was fighting against me. I remember speaking up and saying ok! I was finally ok with the idea of Simon leaving because what once felt like abandonment, started to feel more like freedom. At first, I wondered if I had made the right choice or if I was to blame. I wondered if I should've just given in for the sake of salvaging our matrimony instead of standing firm on how I wanted to be treated. But eventually, that fear turned into sadness.

I mourned the loss of the family dynamic we had built together and I shed tears for the future we planned together that would never exist. Sadness then turned into anger. I was mad that he had chosen to start something new within someone else while we were supposed to be working to fix what we had. I was upset that our marriage had become a storyline and our real lives were casted for public consumption. I found myself being frustrated by the slander, accusations and false narratives. I was overwhelmed with processing the many changes that accompanied our separation; and even drained from it all. I allowed myself to go through the motions and feel all of the many emotions that came with losing love, finding myself and discovering the courage to move on. I gave myself the grace to feel what I felt and eventually the negative emotions turned into relief. I was relieved that I no longer had to be left alone in my marriage. Feelings of gratitude seeped in and I was grateful that God was removing me from a toxic situation that at one point I was fighting to stay in. I was grateful for the opportunity to redesign my life and experience a version of love that didn't hurt, diminish, minimize or drain me. The time I spent in reflection started to pay off because when it was time to walk away, I was able to let go. Surrendering is sweet, not because it's easy, but because it's for your good. When we let go of things that no longer serve us, we make room for relationships and opportunities that inspire us to be our best selves.

Surrender looks different for all of us. If you look at your life close enough, and you examine yourself with honesty, you are bound to uncover things that you are holding onto that are just not good for you. It can be a limiting belief system that prevents you from pursuing your goals and maximizing your potential; or bad habits that hinder your growth. Whether you need to release a relationship that drains your energy, or a faulty belief system that keeps you playing small; what I have learned is that letting go may be difficult but the reward for choosing yourself is well worth the discomfort of surrendering.

Faith in the beauty that your future holds can fuel you to continue to heal in the right direction When you first let go, the first thought that creeps into your mind is whether or not you made the right choice, know that, choosing what's best for you is always the best choice no matter how much it hurts at first. Your heart will heal, your mind will eventually be at ease, you will recover and life will go on even after love.

CHAPTER
FIVE

THE SIN OF SILENCE

"We've been taught that silence
would save us, but it won't"
~Audre Lourde

I chose to remain silent when the news broke that my husband had gotten engaged to my cast mate because I was too stunned and devastated to speak, plus at the time I truly believed that it was the best response. I'm sure you've heard the age old saying that "silence is the best response", but in the case when your public reputation and character are being called into question, there comes a time when your silence becomes complicit and speaking up is not only the right thing to do, but it's the thing you need to do in order to free yourself from the shackles of false narratives. My ex-husband and I had an agreement. We were participating in marriage counseling to work on our marriage over the course of several months. While we were working on our issues, he became absent from our home. He would be away for weeks and then months at a time. Our marriage counseling transitioned from being focused on working out our marital issues, to Uncoupling counseling which was focused intentionally on dissolving our marriage. I cried and pleaded for my husband at the time to come home. I wanted our marriage to work although there were more than enough reasons to justify why I should let it go. Simon needed me to be broken, my healing became a threat to our bond because I was no longer easily manipulated and no longer willing to tolerate things that I had once allowed. I was finding myself, loving myself and embracing the idea of having a dream that I could live out on my own terms. I had never given myself permission to dream, operating in survival mode has a way of blinding you to the possibilities around you and if you're not careful it will completely sabotage your potential. Don't get me wrong. Simon was not all bad. He had several great qualities that made me fall in love with him in the first place. He was generous, ambitious and focused on his goals. I had always admired him for that. But for every great quality that he possessed, there was a toxic trait that would become too much to live with and would ultimately cause the demise of our union. We had an agreement that we were going to be very kind to one another during our divorce proceedings. We agreed that we were going to be amicable and have a very clean divorce. It was after one of our counseling sessions where I broke my silence and unmuted my internal dialogue by speaking up and saying that I was no longer willing to fight for a man who refused to meet me halfway. He wanted me to be more submissive and I needed him to be loyal, trustworthy as well as emotionally and physically present in our marriage. I had been pleading with him for months to come home. He left me alone with my children as well as his own. I was taking care of our home, looking after our children, working on myself, healing, and discovering my worth in his absence. There were many times when I didn't even know where he was. I cried many nights over my marriage until one day the tears stopped flowing. His absence hurt so much at first, but it taught me how to live without him. So, when I spoke up during therapy and demanded that change and compromise be a two-way street, Simon made it very clear that he would not be making any changes. In fact, he didn't feel like he contributed to any of our issues and that was the problem. His unwillingness to partner with me in repairing our relationship allowed me to recognize that if I stayed, our marriage would only serve him and silence me into complacency. It was clear at the end of that session that our differences were irreconcilable. I walked away feeling numb, Simon walked to his car and before leaving the parking lot, he released his statement on social media letting the public know of our divorce. He painted me in such a terrible light in order to compensate for the fact that I was no longer fighting for him. I let him go and just like that, our agreement to be amicable was out of the door. He waged war against me and the battle at hand would be trying to convince the world who I was and how things really transpired. At first all I wanted to do was tell my version of the story. He made it seem as if I had been cheating on him with my assistant and my now fiancé Jaylan, when the truth is that he had abandoned our marriage long before we went public with the news. Jaylan has always been around; Simon was the one who left…it was while he was away and after months of being alone that I discovered that my best friend had been more supportive, caring, and considerate than my missing husband. Our platonic relationship eventually evolved into a romance. Looking back, allowing my feelings to get involved romantically with my best friend wasn't necessarily the right thing to do, but abandoning your wife for months at a time while you travel and jet set with different women wasn't right either. Neither one of us are blameless.

It seemed as if Simon and I went from working together on finding resolution in our marriage whether it was sorting through our issues or processing our separation. Throughout the process, we had been intentional about maintaining a certain level of kindness and respect for one another, so when he started to bash me online and then post his engagement to Porscha right after I was caught off guard, heartbroken, humiliated and devastated. I had come to terms that it was over between us, but to find out that while we were in marriage counseling, and he was gone for months, he had been with other women. The betrayal was heavy. He had never really given our marriage a chance, while we were supposed to be working on us, he was already planning a future with someone else. There were times when I felt powerless. His voice, status, power and the narrative that he created seemed to trump my truth and I found myself wanting to retreat into hiding. It was in hiding that I embarked on healing. I needed to process the pain, the changes, the heartache and the idea of new beginnings for myself. During my lowest moments, Jaylan never left my side. He allowed me to cry, curse, scream, and vent. It held space for me without resentment. No one had ever done that for me before. He made me feel as though I was worthy of being loved even at my lowest point. He reminded me of my strength and he encouraged me to dream and imagine a life for myself. He was there to pick up the pieces of my shattered heart and I fell in love with him for it. Not only was he so good at loving me, he was someone who my children admired, respected and enjoyed being around. He was with us as we navigated the transition of divorce and he made us feel supported during a time that my abandonment issues were greatly triggered.

I was coming into this newfound happiness with an actual mate who I loved and trusted. I was at the crossroads of experiencing the hardest thing of my life, while also learning to embrace the beauty of a healthy attachment. It was like life was testing me to see if I had finally found my voice to stand against things that didn't serve me, and I was able to muster up the courage to finally choose myself by going after what felt good in my soul and not just what looked good. Many people will say that I fumbled the bag, but what I really did was prioritize self-love and healthy love over the illusion of love wrapped in luxury. I felt like I had been put to the ultimate test, and although the entire ordeal was rocky, I made it through.

It's funny how our point of pain can become our point of breakthrough. I released the need to be right and exchanged it for the opportunity to be loved properly. Relationships have a way of revealing to us the areas where we require the most work. My silence was fortified during my moments of sacred stillness. I took time for major self-reflection; this is where silence was my private ally. Silence allowed me to discover and hear my own voice. I had to close my ears to the chatter and block out all the voices, opinions, headlines and assumptions. It was during this time that my sacred silence started to convict me. I thought I was taking the high road, but it turned out that I needed the courage to speak on and stand on my own truth without fear of criticism and misunderstanding. Once I discovered the courage to amplify my own voice, my silence was no longer comforting. The tranquility of blocking out the noise turned into inner turmoil and I was no longer willing to be at war with myself in order to avoid conflict. If you allow the world to drive the narrative for your life, you will get lost in the story that they write for you.

If you find yourself silenced by shame, I hope that you remember that when it comes to matters of the heart, silence is not the best response; truth is. I hope that you remember the power of your own voice and it forces you out of quiet resistance. When you feel as though the opposition before you is a battle too big for you, I hope you remember that faith is your weapon against all adversity. Remain faithful to what feeds your soul, and know that God will lead you through the shadows of fear, uncertainty, doubt and rejection. Trust and honor the small whisper within…that is your inner voice and your intuitive guide. When you silence yourself, you mute the God within you.

CHAPTER
SIX
OWNING MY VOICE

"The one thing that you have that nobody
else has is you. Your voice. Your mind.
Your story and your vision"
~ Anonymous

Owning your voice means that you get to choose what to say and when you want to say it. When shit hit the fan and the news broke about my divorce and pregnancy I was consumed and overwhelmed with the number of headlines, blog posts, D'M's, negative comments, assumptions and speculation. I wasn't prepared for the fast influx of social attacks. I made choices that I believed to be best at that time. Not only did I choose to stay silent first and not share my version of events, but when I finally spoke up, I lied. I told a bold face lie and I'll do it all over again. When Simon announced my pregnancy online, I denied it in order to protect my sanity, my family and my unborn child. I chose my daughter's life over other people's opinions. Everyone seemed to have questions about my pregnancy and the timing of everything. Simon's version of events depicted that he was leaving me because he caught me cheating, with his assistant and was carrying our love child. That wasn't the whole truth.

I admit that I lied about being pregnant, but it was because I was protecting what was dear to me. Simon had attempted to rob me of the opportunity to share my pregnancy on my own terms and he had created a narrative that served his storyline. It wasn't fair that I was robbed of the dignity to announce my daughter's birth. Simon had stolen it from me and he weaponized it when the news broke about his engagement to my classmate when they were both being attacked in the media. He needed to paint a picture and tell a story that would take some of the heat off of him. So, he chose to go public and slander my name, breaking our agreement to move forward with the divorce proceedings in an amicable way.

Simon went so far as to call my best friend at the time with a warning for me. He told my best friend to warn me that if I was to say anything negative about him, his fiancé or their engagement, he would not be able to hold his fiancé back from attacking me. He also threatened to release camera footage from our home of Jaylan entering our gate and driving in his car as evidence to prove his cheating allegations against me.

The truth is that I never cheated on Simon. Jaylan was his personal assistant and always had access to our home as well as the vehicle he was in on the tape that was shared online by Simon. Simon was physically and emotionally absent from our home and our marriage; I simply got tired of begging him to come home. The only thing I was guilty of outside of lying to protect my peace and my privacy was moving on and beating a man at his own game. I was guilty of choosing myself. Choosing me led to the demise of our relationship. When the news hit, yes, I was pregnant with Emma; and I was pregnant by my now fiancé Jaylan, but it wasn't an act of betrayal, it was a matter of personal revolution. Simon wanted to leave and I let him go, letting him go was my sin. Moving on, choosing myself and choosing a life that represented love and not just luxury. If we're being honest, Simon left way before the divorce.

There are several misconceptions, lies, rumors and chatter that have been formed from fragments of information released online. All parties involved know the truth. None of the parties involved are innocent.

We've all done our share of things to hurt one another. But I'm choosing to own my portion of it and no longer be defined by storylines or headlines. I'm choosing to own all of my truth, even if it means being judged, misunderstood or criticized. I believe that when we shine the light on our shadows, what was once in darkness starts to glow and grow. I haven't always made the right decisions; but I forgive myself for making poor decisions that I believe were best for me at the time. I'm grateful for growth and I'm grateful for every person who has played a part in my life. Every relationship, no matter how dysfunctional, helped me discover more about myself. Every tear that was shed represented a lesson that was learned and an opportunity to become clearer about what I want in life, what I deserve and most importantly what deserved me. I'm not here to point fingers or cast blame because none of us are worthy enough to cast the first stone. I hope that this clears the air but my goal was not about merely defending my reputation, but more so to put all of this behind me.

I've moved on and I'm working to finally break the cycle of toxic relationships. The more I heal, the less tolerant I am of things that drain me or bring out the worst in me. I know that I'm not alone. I know that there are so many women out there who may find themselves in situations that minimize them, or in relationships that feed off of their vulnerability. There are so many of us who have found themselves in situations where they've made poor choices based on the poor perception that they have of themselves. If I could tell my younger self anything, I would remind her that she deserves to be loved. I would tell my younger self that she was worthy of good things as a daily affirmation if I knew just how much a diminished and underdeveloped sense of self-worth would lead me down a path of repetitive toxicity. I would look at the young girl who felt alone, violated, scared, hungry, and desperate, and I would comfort her with the reminder that the love she was looking for was something that she shouldn't have to fight for. The love she was searching for would need to be discovered within. I wish I had known to love myself better. I now know that self-love is about choosing partners, situations, relationships, opportunities, environments, beliefs, and habits that nurture my needs and inspire me to become a better version of myself. I've struggled a lot in my life and I don't seek pity because I'm grateful that I survived. I am facing my own truth and I'm willing to stand on it. I am who I am because of what I've endured, the things that I've survived and the decisions that I make daily. As I go forward in my life, raising my children and loving myself more than ever, I hope to encourage other women to begin their healing journey so that they too can do the same. Perfection is not my target. Only progress.

I think that you should give yourself that same grace. Choose to be better, but don't beat yourself up about where you may fall short. On days when you're not your best, give yourself a million second chances. Forgive yourself and focus on progression. When you know your truth and you hide from it, it's a sin and a shame; but when you face it, and embrace it you can learn from it. If I could leave you all with anything it would be to make choices today that your future self will thank you for. Never stay too long in anything that has expired. Knowing when to leave is an art and a virtue. Take responsibility for your life and choose every day to be better.

CHAPTER
SEVEN
REINVENTING MYSELF

"You must learn a new way to think before
you can master a new way to be"
~Marianne Williamson

A major part of my personal evolution was tapping into the healing properties of meditation. I grew up Christian, however, a lot of my family, are Asian Buddhists. Buddhism is all about positivity, self-awareness, self-worth and happiness. One of the biggest differences in prayer practices among Buddhists and

Christians is that when you pray to Buddha, you're not supposed to use the word "I" or "me". These words in prayer are self-focused. Instead of referencing yourself, you're supposed to just ask for what you want, and in turn, you will receive it. I adopted this practice into my meditation because I wanted to make sure that when I was meditating, I was intentionally being very selfless. I wanted to make sure that what I was putting out into the world was exactly what I was preparing for. The art of meditation was the gateway that led me into discovering the power of manifesting. With a clear idea of what I wanted, I was able to align my actions with the things that I was praying for. Deliberate prayers proved to be key in materializing the things that I was visualizing. I remember a day in particular, It was a very sunny, yet beautiful day and I started meditating in front of the window as the sunlight pierced through the glass window and warmed my skin. As I sat in silence, I heard a whisper from within that spoke to me in the most angelic way and told me to paint. I had never painted a day in my life but the call from within led me to buy a canvas, paint and paint brushes. As I stroked the canvas with the brush, I started crying. Each brush stroke unleashed tears of happiness and fulfillment. I felt free for the first time in my life. I remember feeling a sense of liberation and clarity. I had been looking at the world in black and white my entire life, and in that very moment, as I was painting, I saw everything in living color. That was my very first painting and I ended up selling it for $1,200.

Time in solitude allowed me to receive divine downloads that inspired creativity and fortified my healing. This was the catalyst that activated my inner work and self-discovery.

While multitasking the many roles and responsibilities of motherhood and marriage, I slowly drifted away from prioritizing time alone in prayer and meditation. My meditation practices reemerged during the Covid-19 lockdown. Since the whole world was in quarantine, I took it upon myself to go live from Instagram, it was my way of connecting with the outside world. Every single day, I was online, speaking to and sharing with my followers about my life, things I was working on and giving them words of wisdom and inspiration that I had derived from my life experiences. Before I knew it, my following began to grow on Instagram and my numbers on live began to grow as well. I would talk to my audience as I did my makeup while encouraging them to get up, get dressed and look pretty as a means to feel better while being isolated at home. Uplifting others in this way is where I first started to find my voice. I had discovered a new found sense of purpose and fulfillment through encouraging others, but once the lockdown was lifted and everyone was returning to their normal routines, I started to feel as though I was losing myself again. There was a part of me that really enjoyed connecting with others and being able to inspire them to heal, grow, create and be more authentic. So, when the opportunity to join The Real Housewives of Atlanta show opportunity presented itself, Simon encouraged me to join and I originally believed that it would be a great opportunity to reach more people. However, I found that the TV producers were more interested in curating a story that would captivate their audience and fit the narrative they established, even if it wasn't a true reflection of one's reality. The producer's were interested in drama, and if it wasn't there, they would manufacture it for ratings. Tearing down other women went against everything that had served me in my healing process and I ended up quitting the show. The last episode that I ever filmed with the show was the Halloween episode. That night as the film crew was packing up, and the producers were leaving, I literally cursed everybody out told them to get the hell out of my house. That was it for me. I told Simon that we needed to get away and he took me to Costa Rica and New Orleans. We went away for vacation, but it still felt like he wasn't very present. That's when I knew something was wrong. Looking back, I believe that he was already sleeping with Porscha behind my back at the time. The night of the Halloween episode, her energy was different. She wasn't talking to me as she always did. She came in for about 10 minutes before she left. During the time when I was engaged in the infamous altercation that aired on the Halloween episode, Porscha was nowhere to be found, and neither was my husband.

The very first time that we filmed in my home, I remember being upstairs in my closet. It was after we were done filming and all of the women came upstairs to my closet. The film crew and the producers were packing up and preparing to leave. There weren't any cameras upstairs because everyone was just chilling out. Porscha remained downstairs for about thirty minutes while the rest of the ladies joined me upstairs. Simon was the only person downstairs with her at that time. Back then, of course, I didn't think much of it. He was my husband and would have never expected that he would leave me for her. She finally made her way upstairs with the rest of us and she ended up taking a piece of my clothing. She squeezed into my extra small clothing and she left my home with the article of clothing. We were all planning to go out that night but she later informed me that she was no longer able to join us because she and her sister had an appointment with a spiritual worker. Soon after, I started to feel so disconnected from myself. I felt empty and I couldn't understand why. I used to scream to Simon begging him to help me because I didn't know what was wrong. I told him that I felt a strong disconnection from myself and he responded with a blank stare. It was as if he knew something already, but didn't have any answers for me. One day as I sat in my 1000 square foot closet, I cried as I stared at my reflection in the mirror. At some point in time, I stopped crying and I stopped begging for answers and I just started meditating. That was the day that I started coming back in tune myself. Later, Simon would sit me down in our bedroom and tell me that we needed to go to therapy. I was at war with myself because I was still trying to force my marriage to work with somebody who didn't want it to work. While in therapy, I started breaking down and I said out loud that I didn't feel strong enough. A part of me believed, and even expected Simon to console me or even reassure me of my strength or even offer support through empathy. Instead, he looked at me as I wept with frustration and sadness and he said to me with a smile on his face, "That's the Falynn I know". That single act of bliss as I broke down in despair gave me the strength to make the conscious decision to release our marriage. I wiped my tears, looked at the therapist and told her I was no longer willing to sacrifice my strength, sanity or happiness in order to make our marriage work. Simon was only interested in the broken version of me that was susceptible to manipulation and control. He loved me at my worst and couldn't appreciate me at my best. I realized that staying in the marriage would slowly kill the best parts of me.

I chose my own heart and I've been on a journey of nurturing the most sacred parts of myself ever since.

In order to become an improved version of yourself, you must first start with embracing new thoughts and gaining a brand-new perspective. How you see yourself has the greatest impact on the way that you behave in your life, your relationships and in the face of new opportunities. Reinventing yourself is much more than a grand makeover. You can change your hair, you can wear a new dress, you can trade in your Zara pumps for Red Bottoms, but it's not about your shoes or your hair. It's about your heart and your mind, it's about breaking old habits and trying on new beliefs. It's about letting go of who you once were, and then embracing the growing pains. Personal transformation is about pushing through in order to redefine who you can be, and the life that you can have. I wish I could tell you that I have arrived at this grand place of perfection, but that place doesn't exist and I'm sure as hell not chasing it. What I desire above all things is consistent progression in the direction of my best self. That's where I'm headed. That's the path that I'm on. As I continue to heal, prioritize wellness, incorporate self-care, and give myself as many second chances necessary in order to learn what I need to learn.

I have learned to love myself and I've come to terms with my mistakes. If there is anything that I know for sure; it's that real change is not an overnight process. While the choice and the commitment to change may be done in an instance, the process towards it is a series of events that challenge the new you and your ability to break old habits, think new thoughts, and choose people who are good for you so that you can create a life that you love living. It's about letting go of everything that has happened to you and realizing that embracing your future self requires you to focus forward. If you don't take anything else away from this book; I hope that you will walk away with this…. your past does not define you! Abuse does not have to be the theme of your life. At any point you can decide that you want more, that you deserve more, and that you're willing to work to become the version of yourself that can manage more. At the core of reinvention is personal forgiveness, and redemption. It's about accepting who you are, focusing on who you are becoming and releasing who you once were. I am so proud to be where I am today. I'm not exactly where I want to be, but I am navigating at a pace that feels good to my soul and I'm making progress.

This time around I am becoming the architect of my own destiny, deciding who I am, and who I want to be, without the influences of those who only have a version of me in mind that benefits their own needs.

ABOUT THE AUTHOR

F alynn Pina is a devoted mother of three sons and one daughter Troy, Dylan, Liam and Emma. She is a social media influencer, philanthropist who advocates for victims of abuse, women's empowerment speaker and TV personality widely known for her role on the

95

Housewives of Atlanta TV Show on the Bravo network. Falynn was born in Panama City, Florida but raised in Atlanta Ga. She is the second oldest of ten siblings and a savvy business woman who loves creating opportunities for her family.

SINLESS
SELF-CARE JOURNAL

As you turn the last page, I want to honor you and celebrate your growth. Your journey to wellness may look very different from mine, but your personal healing is worth the time, energy and effort required to design a better version of yourself. I want to encourage you to take a few moments to reflect on what you need to let go of, who you need to forgive, how you can love yourself better and why it's important that you decide to no longer stay the same. Every healing journey is different but each one is beautiful in their own way. This is your safe place to open up, be vulnerable and write out your authentic truth. This part of the book is my gift to you. While I am recovering, I am still a work in progress because real healing takes practice. I won't pretend to be perfect or act as if I've arrived. I'm still on my journey and it's a ride that I'm so grateful to be on. Journaling has played such a huge role in helping me check in with myself and I want to extend this opportunity to you as well. The remaining pages of this book is your personal "Sinless Self-Care Journal." It's a reminder to take time for yourself to check in. Are your needs being met? How do you feel? Is there something in your life that you need to pursue or let go? This journal is your sacred place to write without judgment, none of us are blameless and personal truth is sinless.

_____

_____

_____

_____

_____

_____

_____

_____

_____

_____

_____

_____

_____

_____

_____

_____

_____

_____

_____

_____

_____

_____

_____

_____

_____

_____

_____

_____

_____

_____

_____

_____

_____

Printed in Great Britain
by Amazon

14349537R00071